The Being in Humans

poems by

Linda Golden

Finishing Line Press
Georgetown, Kentucky

The Being in Humans

ACKNOWLEDGMENTS

I am grateful for the many people who have been there for me on this journey of creating
this book of poetry. None of this would have happened without their encouragement and
assistance.

First, much kudos to my husband Mike for his patience with my clumsy computer skills,
untangling them to create something that I can be proud of. Also his willingness to read,
reread, and help edit my work. Most of all I appreciate his support of my dreams.

For those teachers who gave me hope that I could write I thank you, especially Jack
Grapes and Ellen Reich. To my writing circle, who listened and gave input as well as
friendship, you have made my life a much richer experience.

Special people who read every word, Saralee Kolitz and Cindy Damassa, were especially
helpful in their comments and most of all their support.

To all the people who allowed me into their lives as a Psychoanalyst, my appreciation
for sharing their lives with me. To my friends and family, my thanks for believing and
supporting me.

Publisher: Leah Maines

Editor: Christen Kincaid

Cover Art: Linda Rae Goldenberg

Author Photo: Myron Michael Goldenberg

Cover Design: Elizabeth Maines

Printed in the USA on acid-free paper.
Order online: www.finishinglinepress.com
               also available on amazon.com

Author inquiries and mail orders:
Finishing Line Press
P. O. Box 1626
Georgetown, Kentucky 40324
U. S. A.

Table of Contents

To my grandchildren
Ian, William, Gwen, Bailey, Lila
Who inspire me every day

The Being in Humans

Constant the noise of the talking voice
Didn't believe it wasn't the real me...at first

Then I began to listen, then to ask
"Who is the one who hears...and what is she listening to"

Garbage, mostly piles of detris disguised as truth
How many judgements are there on the head of a pin
Comments evaluating life, expletives, places, phases of the moon

Feeling the wall of words erecting a barrier between me and experience
Calming me, protecting me...from what

How old was I when the construction commenced
Womb, cradle, language acquisition, past life

I peel away the letters one by one, breathing into spaces
Challenging syllables on their way to words to be silent

Shiver of excitement alternates with shiver of fear
Still, adventure compelling, getting to know the edges of my being

Walking in the world naked brings moment by moment aliveness
To choose to feel or listen without discernment brings deadness

Who Was the Crack in Your World

Who saw you and you knew
    there was nowhere left to hide

        Where were you when the light found you
            cracked you open, no way to be the same

I sit on a couch, the window has no shade, just some plants in a line
    She sits in a chair framed by the glow

        The crack is felt mid-chest, a radiating ache
        Warm as the smile on her face

We don't talk about what is happening, knowing is passed between
    us without words

        Alchemy of body/mind/spirit connection the rarest of gifts
        A sacred honor not sought or expected,
           but a moment of grace

First Touched

Five is old enough to go out the front gate
Up the the stairs next door, sit in the corner
Of the big front room, in a wood cabinet
Opened by the Rabbi, holy books in scrolls
Watch as the bearded old men sway and sing
If I sit there long enough sun comes through
Cut glass windows lighting the room
With a magical glow of all the colors I know
My mommy says a rainbow is light
From the hand of God
I reach back

Who Dances

The moment I became the ink
   fluid flowing falling forward
      finding fear,
         facing it, will I find myself

The shapes of letters dance my loneliness
   waving forms reflect pain
      protrusions of spine spell out
         memories, wishes, wisdom,
            paint pictures of what lies ahead

If I am not afraid
   who am I
      if I no longer pull my hair by root
      only use it to move me up
         to dangle gracefully
            using what follows all that descent
          to grind pigments
            Into pirouettes

Does every curve of letter spell my truth,
   is my vulnerability tempering the core
      the lines on my face
         do they undress, embarrass,
           educate, entertain

Longing clouds, yearning distorts,
   seasons fly, marking me with more awareness
      free when I remember
         obstacles are for my evolution
           then my pen dances with joy

Although fear can take me
for a turn or two
around the floor
I am grateful the muse
moves in me

Who Wrote That on My Page

I see the bow pulled with love
Across the strings and wonder
What force moves it so

Flute put to lips pursed in purpose
Feeling inspiration needed to create
Such soaring notes

Tympani whose muffled sticks
Beat in tune to earth's sway
Keeping time for us all

Just do it they say
Make your own magic
In your own form

No creation can happen unless
I sit with some tool to write
Get out of the way so soul meets paper

Inspiration
Herman Wouk

He is ninety-seven, wry smile, sharp answers still there,
still writing, now more likely to experiment, says he

His wife of over sixty years died not so long ago, he keeps
on keeping on because he wants her to be proud of him

Sitting by the window looking out at their garden, then eyes rest
on the first picture she gave him, he waits for muses to speak

Sunlit autumn day, shadows move across his paper
sometimes his hand moves too, words happen

He calls himself lazy, only 13 novels in 67 years
Careful crafting can take a long time

Arthritic joints complain in efforting, he moves anyway
sure in the knowledge he is fulfilling his destiny

I sit writing, wondering when I get to be finished,
removed from my post, anointed done, 97 far away

What is my fate, where does that sudden intake of
air come from, then relief of soul sounding its screed

I long for his sureness, his fluency, his knowing
May I wake tomorrow to as clear a view of my path

Rewind

Why would I want to revisit the scene
Reminding myself of such old pain
Yet I send myself down a black hole where wait
Dark nights, visages, violent plays best forgotten

A small child waits for my return to carry her
From this hellhole, this time taking back maps,
Light, stories to tell

Having survived the first round alone,
Back this time, older, wiser,
Making sure to have a witness,
Who will hand hold, whisper comfort

Still the creepy shadows have not lost their ability to
Frighten nor the clanging sounds their power to startle
Some bravery still required, a worthy trip nevertheless
When it first happened I didn't know how to pray or ask
For help or bind my wounds or leave a trail of crumbs

Now few stories surprise, range of human creativity
For harm still amazing, depravity ongoing darkness
What astounds me is what some of us are able to craft
From the rubble

Secret

Choose the best thing not the first thing
That pops into your head, nobody told me
Value always went to the fastest
Robbing me of the best thing about me
Answers gained in reflection
Years went by before I knew to take a breath
Before I opened my mouth and said
Whatever was in there
Wars were started for less
Wounds went deep when carefully aimed
Instead of a carefully planned comment
Bloodshed became the mark of courage
Now prize non-surgical techniques
Bruising becomes a mark of clumsiness
Heart plus brain always the best strategy

Heart Song

Play me down your river, rock me gently as we go
Take me with you, hold my hand, open me

Craft me a vessel of reeds, a lullaby of birdsongs
Show me the way back home by a trail of revelations

I know you do not mock my longing to understand
Hold your stars still enough for me to touch their light

Show me the budding in all that lives
Remind me of the flowering that surrounds me

My hands move across the keys of life
Sometimes I hear beauty in the music,

Shining orbs move across sky, visible or not
It is always there, whether or not it casts shadows

Remind me how to pray, how to be quiet so I can hear
Remind me that I am counseled to bless myself

Do not let me go without using my pen to write from my heart
What I know when I remember who you are, who I am

How Will I Grow

Built to move, mature, make,
Most of the time dragging myself,
Slowing down out of fear
Moving anyway because once in a while
I get it

By force or grace, how to be present
To choose to molt graciously
Or lull, lazy, silent, frozen
Requiring crisis to shake me loose
So I get it

How to accept the block in my way
Is part of what grows me
It has its purpose, it is not a lie
It is just another signpost to steer by
So I can get it

I only grow if I own my journey
To what is sacred
What makes me weak
What makes me strong, it's all the same
For this moment I got it

Spirit's Emergency

Almost
As if someone is whispering
in my ear, wake up
I turn over, pull the pillow
over my head

No use
I have run from the
blank sheets to long

I stumble out of bed,
flashlight in hand
There sits my journal
Fumble about for a pen,
tears follow as I
find my way home

Layers of armor
melt in the heat
where passion meets
the paper

Excavation proceeds
knit brows soften
memory moves hand,
feelings chase it
across the pages

I can breathe again

Good Enough

Remember Mexico City, the path to the cathedral
How I cried to see people on their knees
Going for miles to seek redemption, ask for help
I wanted no part of a God that asks such leave
Poor souls, whose clergy recommends that display.

Many times in my life I have gone down on my knees
Forced there by serious situations to feel time out of time
To return to the awe of the little girl reaching for rainbow
To be in touch with the divine, to revel in the connection
To honor something greater than myself, in the quiet
To know that this is part of myself that makes me whole
No bloody display or degradation of the soul is necessary

Don't Be Sorry, Be Different

The trouble is you can't unring a bell
You can say you are sorry, even mean it
The information gets passed on anyway
The cumulative effect wears down
Pain settles in the body in spaces that are
Supposed to be flexible, tighten under assault
Freeze over time until thawing ceases to occur
This is not a choice but the bodies reaction
Hardwired for survival unconscious reflexive
Only hard work digging in the muck of the
Previously unexamined mire can set free
The choice to reengage, hard to muster
Not to choose unthinkable

Dark Places

I know when I write down the bones
Close as I can without breaking them,
Then I have your attention.

Don't try to engage me with any less in you
Outside the skin is a gift to no one, nor neck up
Dazzle detracts from depth

I'll even bleed for you, bind my wounds,
Cry out loud or weep softly.
I am not brave, I am on a mission

To tell my story, so you can find your way there
Feel something, know something, find your way back.
Tell it to someone so they can walk their own way out.

Sharing is the only real teaching we have
My story is harder to tell than you know
Please don't make me go to that dark space alone.

Now

Is that all there is
That one foot in the air while I walk
Space between then and second footfall

Can I make it up the hill
Will worrying about it take me out of the now
Does it matter where I stop, or does judgement efface

If I feel broken
Is everything else in pieces, is the whole in every part
Where do I go to heal, or in now is everything always fine

Philosophy meets injured edges
Hard knocks held in the grip of doctrine bleed the same
Staying in present, panacea or pablum, illusion or illumination

When alone in darkness of the underbelly of my mind
Breathing through tight spaces
I find bits of peace

No More

Soft in the quiet folds of the labyrinth of her mind
Lies the truth unbidden, left buried behind glossy
Bits of disguise parading as good intention

Crumpled beneath decades of doubt, self-flagellation
Broken mirror of the world reflection, declarations
To the contrary, smoke of thousands of good deeds
Verity will out.

Excavation, layers of inane arcane insane
Exposing tarnished shards, fragments of unfinished songs
Tatters of forgotten dances, cracked casings of
Dreams, wishes, prayers
Languishing in limbo for lack of will, fortitude, bravery

She loosens her death grip on the shutters of her soul
Facing the very real ripples in a facade so carefully made
Tendrils of imperfection no longer cripple, wonder at the hold
So tenacious it all but blocked life's breath, love's truth
Waking from such a nightmare she walks naked into the day

Healing Old Wounds

We have the luxury of thinking about reunion for a few months
    What do I want, what do you want, what do we need

We grew up cousins, but really we were more like sisters
    Family tragedy set us on course to this long separation

In our dotage we have another chance, another choice
    Time is slipping away from us with astounding speed

Chance led me to contact you, who knows why that happened
    I sat for many hours before I pushed the right keys, buttons

For our beloved Auntie, I said to myself, but really it was for me
    Remember, remember, remember, so many memories wash over

So many pictures in my mind, in albums, on walls
    Still a watery sore place where our sharing used to be

We have both accomplished much, far from our storm-tossed
    Impoverished unconscious immigrant grandparents

We survived much from the legacy that scarred our fathers
    Physically, emotionally, ruins splashed to next generations

What will we do with our chance to turn that tide to choose a new path
    Now becoming part of my daily prayer, choose peace, make peace,
        Choose peace.

Hers

She used to wait for the next turn of the wheel
Sure that whatever came next had to be better

Now it is clear to her it is all the same
All that happens has to do with who she is
not where the ride is heading

There is no running away from lessons
She now knows they are why we are here

Clock ticking reminds her every minute counts
how many opportunities wasted, choices missed,
what consequences meted, how much blood paid

She had wished for a different destiny
not understanding the perfections of her own

Her hand reaches for his arm as they go to sleep,
her life contains all she needs

God, When I Die

When I die I want them to sing
Amazing Grace, twice, once for me
And once for them.
I have not always lived this life
Gracefully, but I have been
Willing to learn eventually.
I want them to know I believe in God
That whatever has brought my end
I have been returned to
Amazing Grace.
That I love all who come to say
Goodbye and all who passed before
That we will all say hello again,
Dance again, love again.

Going Home

Home is not a place but a state of mind, heart, feelings
born of history mixed with memory, faulty or not, flashes of pictures
folded into a batter baked in an oven of time

I still call Topanga home even though I haven't lived there for
nearly five years. Our ashes will be scattered in the park behind
where we lived, fell apart, came back together

Then we forged a bond that will last beyond our corporeal presence,
circles of grey matter, yours and mine, and our beloved dogs,
joined in an ephemeral set of spheres

Seeping back into the earth to nourish the ancient oaks that wrapped
their limbs around our abode, our hearts, our souls, sheltering us from
Baking sun, whipping rain, loaning a place to lean, talk, read or muse

Then we will be home

Autumn of Our Lives

The hunter's moon followed me home last night
    Golden orb chased me around mountain curves
        Playing hide and seek behind craggy peaks
            Making modern art framed by ancient oaks

Today a bright fall day, winding through the canyon
    In daylight only shadows pursue me around corners
        Cobalt sky dotted with wispy strands
            Leaves turning their fall jewel tones

Nip in the air a surprise after
    A day of Indian summer weather
        Toasty yesterday, thoughts of cold weather food
            Far away, we sit on our patio, sunhats essential

Where has this year gone
    Gone to bury my brother
        Gone to gray hair
            Gone to surgery for new eyes
                Gone to shrinking circles of friends
                    Shorter walks, smaller meals, earlier bedtimes
                        Never far, gratitude for memory and a rich life

Web of Life

Lines are all around me, some to honor, some to sing,
some to break, some to attach to kites and fly
Most unfurl to find their origin or their end
Many need to be reknit, new raiment that is better fit
I go about taking cables, threading long needles
through color and texture, some patches remain untouched
attached whole to be remembered, others unwind
to be recalled anew or fashioned for another to wear
Nothing wasted, all is the stuff of which we are fashioned
Remaking it is our task
Yesterday I pulled a thread that bound a piece of soul
left over from an old nightmare, twisted it with last nights
moonlight and made a new scarf to warm me
Today the skein is made of hope for tomorrow's clarity

We Love Because We Can Forgive

Somewhere between before and after,
Around the corner from now, because of him
She wanted to die as much as she wanted to live,
It wasn't so much a choice as a wish to disappear
To find a place where walking through walls was possible
Home would become a passing cloud, or heart of a daisy
Tears like so many white petals, elective, pain optional,
Heart armored by betrayal, responsively glacial

Hung like some kind of ornament betwixt here and never
Viewing the carnage of life lived on the half shell
She found her vision wrapped in music of spheres
Tiny light flickering, then star bright binding her back
To this world, viewed from afar, its humanness
Urging her to call herself beloved, lightning informing
Somewhere in forgiveness, she grants him the same

What Is Important

We live upstairs
Twenty steps and a world away
Granny apartment retreat.
We listen as piping voices
Ask to come visit
A bright spot in our day.
What price this proximity
Precarious walk of wishes
Versus reality
Deeply breathing
Versus knee jerk response
Fragile bonds reinforced
With each kindness.
Sharing wonder
Generation after generation
Come see the crystal spiderweb
Can we make cookies
Stand on my feet, let's dance
A small hand in mine.
We walk through days
As if they will never end
And remember only occasionally
That one day small hands will match ours
Then in an instant we may be gone

The Fates

Biggest opponent...an aching heart
    Carried as treasured wound
        Blocking the way to destiny

Watched generations...wedded to this plan
    Sure in knowledge of its value
        Blinded to its cost

Buried under layers...stories touted righteousness
    Pictures of hollow-eyed martyrs
        Revered in hallowed halls

Little light glimmered to illuminate flaws
    Fallacy multiplies in moldy corners
        Shrouded velvet robes or scented incense

Now I find the holy
    In forests where sunlight filters
        Luminous patches find shimmery blossoms

Now I find sacred
    In the smiles of children
        The arm-in-arm of grey-haired ones

Now I find grace
    In waking to another gift of day
        And a sunset that finds today I have made peace

Move

Drift
Out of this jumble
Something will evolve

How brave are you, am I
To allow unfolding
Moving only from source

Letting it become itself
Not a construct
The wind is flowing...fly free

What happens
Living the artist in me
Shining beam in dark spaces

Broken pieces
Are they meant to be
Or be hidden away

Do I open my mouth
To the water from the heavens
As well as salty tears

Welcome conflict as teacher
Rejoice in banging heads
Or hide my face in shame

Black and white of me
Moving free to music of soul
Or dressing in a corset of fear

Syncopated rhythms can
Break old straight-jacketed form
Can I let it happen...can I let myself be

I awaken every sunrise anew
Faced with the same choice
Same ritual of finding self

Linda Golden was born in Brooklyn, her family moved to California when she was 4. She grew up in the Los Angeles area where she still lives.

Early on she was fascinated by rituals around religion. Drawn by the energy before she understood what that was. She used to sit on the floor watching participants entranced. Even when she traveled she was drawn to houses of worship or found that feeling in nature. She eventually ended up living in Topanga, a rural mountain community, for over thirty years.

Because of a family tragedy, when she was a teenager, she sought to understand what had happened. The study of psychology lead her through school. Some answers were found there. Still something was missing. She gravitated back to things spiritual. She found the marriage of psychology and spirituality to be helpful to her as well as the people she worked with. Linda came to see that a psychological view of history is helpful to people in order for them to understand the patterns in their lives. Healing their life in the present was aided by the precepts of a spiritual approach. Even when she took advanced training to be a Psychoanalyst, she found adding other level of awareness useful.

She is married to Mike, her childhood sweetheart. They met when she was fifteen, he seventeen. They grew together, sometimes unevenly, each finding their own paths, sharing many others. They have two children, both married, with five grandchildren between them.

In retirement they moved to a granny apartment in their son and daughter-in-law's house. This multigenerational home is also occupied by three grandchildren. Mike and Linda visit with their Northern California contingent often.

She and Mike explore painting, sculpture, enjoy world traveling. Writing in a group setting has been one of the treasures of this time of life. Linda is grateful for the support and inspiration she has received from her fellow writing travelers. She has been published in print and online in numerous publications. All of her interests, passions, come together in this, her first book.

www.ingramcontent.com/pod-product-compliance
Lightning Source LLC
LaVergne TN
LVHW051612080426
835510LV00020B/3260